Night's Can

A play

Hazel Wyld

Samuel French—London
New York-Toronto-Hollywood

ISBN 0 573 12177 X

Please see page iv for further copyright information

CHARACTERS

Fizz
Frank
Man
Girl
Peter

COPYRIGHT INFORMATION
(See also page ii)

For Gary, Debbie, David, Andrew, Jackie
and John -
my best and original creations

NIGHT'S CANDLES

A rambling garden. There is a table with a teapot, teacups, and a small bell on it. There is a chair by the table and a bench DL

As the CURTAIN *rises, the Lights come up, filtering in through trees and shrubs*

Fizz, an old lady, is sitting at the table. She is dreaming

The sound of bird-song. Fizz comes to with a start

Fizz (*sighing*) I must have dropped off. (*She stretches*) Oh, lovely. Tea! (*She feels the pot*) Mmm. Still hot. It can't have been here long.

A lark sings. Fizz listens, her head to one side; she quotes softly

> "It was the nightingale and not the lark
> That pierc'd the fearful hollow of thine ear.
> Nightly she sings on yon pomegranate tree.
> Believe me, love, it was the nightingale."

Pause

Frank (*off*) "It was the lark, the herald of the morn,
   No nightingale."
Fizz (*startled*) What the——

Frank enters L. *He pauses. He is very old*

Frank "Look love, what envious streaks
      Do lace the severing clouds in yonder east.
      Night's candles are burnt out——"
Fizz (*looking at him crossly*) Oh, shut up. Never mind night's
      candles. If anything's burnt out round here it's you. You're too
      old to cast for Romeo. It's too late! Fifty years too late!
Frank If I were not a gentleman I would answer that with cruelty
      but truth... Hallo, Fizz.
Fizz (*annoyed*) What are you doing here?
Frank May I sit down? (*He sits*) I was about to ask you the same
      question. Is that tea fresh?
Fizz I suppose you followed me here!
Frank Certainly not. (*He pours himself some tea*)
Fizz (*getting annoyed*) I hope you don't expect me to believe that
      it's sheer coincidence. I come away for a few days' peace and
      quiet...
Frank When?
Fizz When what?
Frank When did you come away for a few days' peace and quiet?

The lark sings again as Fizz makes no reply

Frank (*reasonably*) After all, if you came here first there might
      be some justification for thinking I followed you. I didn't, but
      there might be some justification... On the other hand, if I got
      here first then I might well accuse you of following me.
Fizz That'll be the day.
Frank You have been known to follow me.
Fizz (*coldly*) Really! When?
Frank (*musing*) On several occasions: once to St Moritz, another
      time to Paris.

Fizz Well, if you're going to go back forty years…

Frank Another time to Athens.

Fizz I did not follow you to Athens—you followed me.

Frank Come to think of it—you're quite right. You were having an affair with that dago harpist.

Fizz I was not! And even if I had been it was hardly your business. We'd been divorced for three years.

Frank (*comfortably*) Maybe so… Nevertheless, you were supposedly too ill to go on tour with *The Merchant of Venice*. Naturally, I was somewhat annoyed to find you swanning off to Athens with an Italian gigolo with acne.

Fizz He didn't have acne. Those were smallpox scars. (*Dreamily*) He was very romantic—like Lord Byron. Italians are romantic; all those dark curls and soulful eyes.

Frank Lord Byron was Irish.

Fizz English!

Frank Irish.

Fizz Well, it's beside the point. I meant romantic like Byron—not Italian like Byron.

Frank He might well have been romantic looking, but he was a raving poof.

Fizz He most certainly was not! As a lover he was—superb. I remember the first time we——

Frank I didn't mean the Italian. I was referring to Byron. I was not inviting the sordid details of your fling with a third-grade harp player. I didn't wish to hear them at the time and I certainly don't wish to hear them now. That dago nearly ended up playing his harp at the pearly gates.

Fizz Stop calling him a dago. It implies I paid him! You know as little about romance as you do about Byron, which is sod-all. I know for a fact Byron was an English gentleman.

Frank Irish—and no gentleman.

Fizz He was English. You're thinking of Yeats.

Frank They were both Irish.

Fizz Tosh! Anyway, I notice you've managed to adroitly change the subject as usual! Why are you following me around? I'm seventy-five years old; you surely haven't come here to check up on me again. I'm a little old to be sneaking off for a weekend of illicit passion.

Frank You're seventy-eight, and I didn't follow you here. Is there any more tea in that pot?

Fizz Just answer the question! What are you doing here?

Frank I've been ill. I came away for a rest.

Fizz (*cruelly*) Yes. I heard the National had dropped you. I saw your reviews—you were totally unsuited for the part of Fopping. If you'd asked my advice…

Frank I was not totally unsuited. And the National did not drop me—they released me from my contract. I had a virus, I was very ill, it was touch and go.

Fizz Tony Hope said you had no talent for Restoration comedy; you should stick to what you know.

Frank Tony Hope is another pansy.

Fizz Well, he doesn't fancy you, that's for sure. He said you walked like an egg-bound chicken.

Frank (*coldly*) I read the review, thank you.

Fizz You haven't the figure for tights—you never did have—you have spindly thighs.

Frank I shall treat that remark with the contempt it deserves. Perhaps you'd like to explain what you're doing here, instead of cross-questioning me like a prosecuting counsel. You managed to skate round the question of when you arrived rather skilfully.

Fizz (*hesitantly*) Well… To tell you the truth—I'm not sure. I seem to have forgotten.

Frank Don't be ridiculous.

Fizz No, truly. I can't remember a thing prior to your arrival. I'm not even sure where we are!

Frank Well, that's simple enough. We're at…

A brief pause. More bird-song is heard

Fizz Well?

Frank (*slowly*) Dashed if I can remember the name of the place either.

Fizz Don't be stupid! You always have to have what I've got. If I had a sore throat, you had tonsillitis. If I had a cold, you had the flu; when I got sciatica, you slipped a disc. Now I can't even have senile dementia on my own. Thank God we never had any children! How would you have topped that, I wonder?

Frank I'm serious. I can't remember a thing about this place. (*He gets up and looks around*) Is it an hotel? Or are we house guests somewhere?

Fizz (*slowly*) You are joking, aren't you?

Frank (*slowly*) No.

Fizz You're frightening me. Stop it.

Frank Let's take this slowly. (*He sits again*) What is the last thing you can remember? Take your time—don't panic.

Fizz (*acidly*) I never panic. (*She thinks aloud*) The last thing I remember… Well, of course—I was—it was—I must have… The last thing I remember is—sitting here listening to the birds and thinking how peaceful it was.

Frank Who brought the tea?

Fizz (*crossly*) I don't remember. No… (*Thinking*) It was here— the tea was here already. I was sitting here and the tea was here, waiting for me. It was hot—it couldn't have been here long.

Frank What can you remember before sitting here? Try and think back. Before you came into the garden.

Fizz I remember… (*Slowly*) I remember… Hearing you were ill—in hospital. That's right, James Godfrey came to see me, at home. He said you were in hospital and… And then it's all confused. Oh, this is silly.

Frank No, no. Let me think what I can remember. I was ill, in hospital. It was some sort of virus. I thought I was going to die. You know the sort of thing—couldn't get my breathing. Then, I... It was...

Fizz What?

Frank (*uncertainly*) I remember walking through those trees and seeing you sitting there...

Fizz (*frightened*) I don't like this!

Frank (*jokingly*) Perhaps we're dead!

Fizz Both of us? Don't be stupid. Anyway, I was perfectly all right. You were the one who was at death's door.

Frank Is that a bell?

Fizz What?

Frank There, on the table. Is it a bell?

Fizz (*puzzled*) Yes. How odd—I didn't notice it before.

Frank Don't be dramatic. It hasn't just appeared like a genie from a bottle. It was there earlier. Ring it.

Fizz (*scared*) Shall I?

Frank Well, what else is it for? (*Lightly*) If an angel with large wings and a halo comes in—we're in dead trouble.

Fizz Or a harp!

Frank If anyone comes in with a harp, you're the only one in trouble. That affair with the music man was supposed to be long over.

Fizz You're such a fool. I am an old lady! How many times do I have to remind you? I haven't had an affair for... Oh, it must be—ten years.

Frank (*affronted*) Ten years! Good God! I thought twenty-five at least. It's obscene, a woman of your age.

Fizz (*ringing the bell*) Shut up.

A chorus of bird-song

The Lights change

Girl enters. She is dressed in clothes reminiscent of the Thirties. She stands left of Fizz and Frank. They see her but she is oblivious to them

Girl I feel such a fool. Supposing he doesn't turn up.
Fizz (*whispering*) Who is she?
Girl "Meet me by the bandstand" indeed. So sure of himself!

Music plays: a jolly brass band

Fizz Oh my God!
Frank What? What is it?
Fizz Shush! Listen.

Man enters. He is young, wearing a boater and a striped blazer

Man Sorry!
Girl Oh, hallo!
Man Sorry to be late.

Girl feigns indifference

Girl Are you late?
Man Shall we walk?
Girl If you like.

They stroll a few steps

Man Would you like to sit? (*He gestures to the bench*)
Girl All right.

They sit

Man Your audition—I thought you were marvellous.

Girl (*pleased*) Really?

Man Marvellous!

Girl I don't have your experience, of course. Or training.

Man You don't need it. You're a natural actress.

Girl I don't know what to say.

Man I say! Would you care for some tea?

Girl Tea? Did you bring a hip flask?

Man No, no. Perhaps... I mean... I thought... The Corner House?

Girl That would be nice.

They exit

Fizz and Frank watch them go

Fizz (*frightened*) What's happening?

Frank Dashed if I know! Who were they?

Fizz Oh, Frank!

Frank rings the bell again

Frank Service is dashed slow here.

The Lights change

> *Man enters. He is now in shirt sleeves and carries a script. He comes down stage slightly. Shielding his eyes, he calls out to someone unseen*

Man Can we have the lights down a bit? (*He moves to the front of the stage and peers out into the audience*) Jeremy? Wake up, for God's sake. Bring the lights down! (*He paces a bit, consulting his script*) Let's take it from "Fetch Desdemona hither". (*He clears his throat self-consciously*)

"Ancient, conduct them, you best know the place:
And till she come, as faithful as to heaven
I do confess the vices of my blood,
So justly to your grave ears I'll present
How I did thrive in this fair lady's love,
And she in mine."

Girl enters. She is tying a silk robe round her and looks flustered

Girl I was trying to have my lunch.

Man Look, darling, I think we need to——

Girl (*snapping*) Eat!

Man Just run through scene——

Girl Just us?

Man Well... The others have gone for lunch.

Girl How inconsiderate of them! And after a mere five hours rehearsal.

Man I just thought——

Girl Honestly, darling.

Man I'm sorry. I just want this to be wonderful. Our first joint venture. Well... As husband and wife.

Girl (*softening*) It will be wonderful. How could it fail with you... But honestly, darling. You're such a perfectionist.

They kiss

Man I want everyone to know what a marvellous Shakespearian actress you are.

Girl I just want to be famous.

Man You will be—we'll both be famous.

Girl Like Jean Harlow.

Man (*stupefied*) Jean Harlow?

Girl (*dreamily*) Or Greta Garbo.

Frank Good grief! Does this seem familiar to——
Fizz Shush!
Man Darling, we're actors, not film stars.
Girl Can't we be both?
Man (*laughing*) Absolutely not!
Girl Wouldn't you like to go to Hollywood?
Man Good grief, no!
Girl You don't see yourself as Clark Gable?
Man I most certainly do not.
Girl (*laughing*) You're such a snob!
Man (*relieved*) And you're a tease.
Girl Darling!

They embrace

Man I'm going to take you to eat.
Girl No, no, we'll work.
Man (*firmly*) We'll eat.

Girl starts to protest but he puts his hand gently over her mouth

We'll eat.

They exit, arm in arm

Slight pause

Frank What's happening?
Fizz It's us. The way it was—once.
Frank I don't understand what's happening.
Fizz Perhaps we're dreaming.
Frank Both of us?
Fizz Am I in your dream? Or are you in mine, I wonder?

Frank Well, if it's your dream, I wish you'd wake up. I'm not enjoying it one little bit.

Fizz I've read books about this. Your past life flashing before you.

Frank I thought that was when you drowned.

Fizz (*flatly*) We're dead.

Frank (*hopefully*) Maybe it's those funny cigarettes you smoke. I'm in your hallucination.

Fizz Those "funny" cigarettes are Turkish!

Frank sniffs in a meaningful manner

I know you never believed it. But they were Turkish, I swear it on——

Frank Please don't say it.

Fizz We must be dead. I'm going to be frightfully depressed if we've got to sit through our past lives.

Frank (*heavily sarcastic*) Yours will be enthralling, I'm sure.

Fizz (*abruptly*) You should have come to America with me.

Frank What?

Fizz When I went to Hollywood, you should have come too.

Frank I'm an actor, not a bloody film star.

Fizz You're a snob. Acting is acting. Film making is just more lucrative, that's all.

Frank Prostitution.

Fizz Oh, don't be a fathead. I made a fortune.

Frank You spent a fortune.

Fizz You were jealous; no-one in Hollywood saw you as star material.

Frank Any fool can be an actor on film, you only say one line at a time.

Fizz Shows how much you know about it.

Frank I had my chances. I happen to prefer real acting, on the stage.

Fizz Perhaps you were right. For films you need—sex appeal.
Frank (*offended*) I had sex appeal.
Fizz No, you didn't. Not really. You had—presence.
Frank I'm ringing that bell again. (*He rings the bell*)

Pause

> *Man enters. He is wearing a dressing-gown and holding a phone into which he speaks*

Man That is wonderful… Truly wonderful… We'd be thrilled…
Yes, by all means… Saturday after the show.

> *Girl enters. She is wearing a négligé*

Girl Honestly, darling, every time I walk into a room, you're on
the phone. We're supposed to be at Phil's by——
Man Shh! (*Into the phone*) Marvellous… See you Saturday…
Bye.
Girl Saturday?
Man My darling, that was no less than Al Cohen.
Girl And?
Man Stratford, here we come!
Girl Is that what he said?
Man As good as… He's coming to see us Saturday week; he
wants us to dine with him after the last show. (*He looks at his
watch*) Look at the time! Why aren't you dressed? We're
supposed to be at Phil's by one.

Man exits

Girl (*calling after him*) Well, honestly! I was trying to tell you
that! Darling, do listen. I'm not sure we should commit
ourselves to a long term contract. Darling… Do listen!

Girl exits

Frank Were we really so sweet to each other all the time?

Fizz We were very young.

Frank (*sighing*) Yes. When did the rot set in?

Fizz (*icily*) When you changed.

Frank I changed? I like that. You were the one with all the silly ideas.

Fizz I never wanted to be a classical actress, I told you that right from the start.

Frank Well, I admit you were lightweight, but I——

Fizz Lightweight!

Frank You had no ambition.

Fizz (*furiously*) I like that! I had no ambition! You were the stick-in-the-mud who wouldn't change.

Frank Why should I have changed? I never pretended to be anything but what I was—an actor.

Fizz Even Laurence Olivier went to Hollywood.

Frank Only for the money.

Fizz You don't know that. Anyway, would it have hurt you to have gone for the money?

Frank I might have changed my mind until I saw what it did to you.

Fizz Indeed? And what precisely did it do to me?

Frank It turned you into a loose woman.

Fizz No, dear, you did that.

Frank I did? And how, pray, did I manage to achieve that?

Fizz When you started behaving like a Victorian husband.

Frank Victorian husband indeed! As I remember——

Fizz You started accusing me of having affairs with all my leading men.

Frank You *were* having affairs with all your leading men.

Fizz No, I wasn't. Not at first. Not until you started accusing me.

Frank You put me second to your career.

Fizz I don't see it like that. You tried to hold me back.

Frank Well, anyway, you got what you wanted. You became a "film star".

Fizz I certainly did. And you hated it, you hated my success.

Frank I hated what it turned you into.

Fizz Well, then, you were well rid of me.

Frank As it turned out—I probably was.

Fizz And I certainly have no regrets.

Frank rings the bell loudly. They glare at each other

The Lights change

> *Girl enters. She is dressed in a slip and is holding a telegram*

Girl I don't believe it. I bloody don't believe it! (*She does a dance of delight, whirling round the stage*) Hollywood! My God! Hollywood! They want me! They want *me!* (*She hesitates, then looks at the telegram again*) They want *me*... They don't want us. (*She hugs the telegram to her breast*) I have to go. This is what I wanted, what I always wanted.

> *Man enters. He is once again in shirt sleeves. He moves down stage from the girl and faces the audience*

Man It was what she wanted. To be a star. A film star. I thought she wanted to be an actress. The theatre... (*Contemptuously*) Hollywood!

Fizz I can't bear it. Not again.

She rises and moves to Girl who cannot see her

You mustn't go.

Girl (*turning to Man*) Don't you see? It's Hollywood! It's fame, glamour, money.

Man What about us?

Girl You can come... We can both go.

Fizz No. He won't go. It will finish you both. You mustn't go!

Frank moves down stage to Fizz

Frank I thought you had no regrets.

Fizz (*passionately*) Regrets! It destroyed us!

Frank You got what you wanted. Fame, glamour...

Fizz You left me.

Frank No, my dear, you left me.

Man I don't want to go.

Girl (*slowly*) I do. (*She reaches out to Man*)

Man turns around and walks off. She follows slowly

Peter enters. He is dressed as a butler and looks rather distinguished

Peter (*to Fizz*) You rang, madam? (*He bows*)

Frank (*relieved*) Well! Now it all falls into place. We're in a Coward comedy!

Fizz (*bewildered*) What is happening?

Peter You rang, I believe.

Fizz Who are you?

Peter My name is Peter, madam.

Frank I think I'd rather it was James.

Fizz What?

Frank Peter—you know. It has—(*he lowers his voice*) connotations.

Fizz What does?

Frank Peter! Pearly gates, etc.
Fizz Oh! (*She looks doubtfully at Peter*)

Peter looks back without expression

Frank Is this an hotel?
Peter No, sir.
Fizz A rest-home?

Peter shakes his head

Pause

Frank (*abruptly*) Look here. Where are we?
Peter (*sighing*) I hoped you wouldn't ask that.
Fizz (*fearfully*) Why?
Peter Everyone does. It gets monotonous.
Frank Everyone?
Peter Everyone. I keep hoping. Someday someone will put the
    question differently.
Frank Look here——
Fizz (*frightened*) Don't!
Frank Fizz!
Fizz Don't ask him. I don't want to know.
Frank Darling, we have to know. Sooner or later. I'd rather get
    it over with. We're dead. That's it, isn't it?
Peter I prefer "passed over". Dead has such a final ring, I always
    think.
Frank "Passed over" sounds pretty final to me.
Fizz (*bursting into tears*) I don't want to be dead. I'm not ready
    to die.
Frank She doesn't mean that. She just likes to feel she controls
    the decisions.

Peter Well, in a manner of speaking, she did.

Frank (*horrified*) You don't mean... I mean, it wasn't... She didn't... (*He mimes a noose round the neck*)

Peter (*shocked*) Dear me, no, we take a very poor view of that kind of thing. We have to alter the records, you see; it causes endless problems.

Frank (*intrigued*) Really? What kind of problems?

Fizz (*sniffing*) Oh, what does it matter what problems? I don't understand anything. This is all ridiculous. I don't believe any of it! Is it some kind of practical joke? I mean if you are making fools of us and we're not dead at all I'm going to be absolutely furious, I don't mind telling you.

Peter (*shocked*) It is most certainly not a practical joke.

Fizz Well, I don't see how I can be dead; I wasn't even ill!

Peter It was rather romantic really. You heard your husband was dying and you had a heart attack and actually got here five minutes earlier than he did. We found it rather touching.

Frank (*annoyed*) I don't find it in the least bit touching! She always upstaged me in life, now it turns out she even upstaged me at death's door.

Fizz (*wistfully*) What a pity we won't get to read the reviews.

Peter It was billed as the love story of the century!

Frank That's ridiculous! Absolute claptrap; the popular press, I suppose. You seem to have forgotten we were divorced. I am actually her ex-husband.

Peter (*loftily*) We don't take any notice of that kind of thing here.

Fizz So where is here?

Peter (*surprised*) The hereafter, of course.

Fizz Are we in heaven?

Peter You may call it anything you wish. We call it the hereafter, it seems an appropriate name.

Frank So now what?

Peter I beg your pardon?

Frank What next? I mean, I rather thought heaven was a beautiful garden and one's loved ones waiting to greet you and all that kind of stuff.

Peter We have a complication.

Fizz Is that the royal "we" by any chance?

Peter A technical hitch you might say.

Frank What kind of technical hitch?

Peter Very rare, I'm relieved to say.

Fizz (*laughing*) You mean I belong up here and Frank... (*She gestures downwards*)

Frank You must be joking! More like the other way around.

Peter No, no... The problem is—more delicate.

Fizz Yes?

Peter Well... You aren't actually... That is... It's all a little premature...

Fizz Premature?

Peter Your being here, madam. Prematurely... So to speak.

Fizz What do you mean, "Prematurely"? I mean, I'm either dead——

Peter Passed over.

Fizz —or I'm not.

Peter Well, that's the whole point. You're not.

Fizz But I'm here. I must be.

Peter I'm afraid you shouldn't be... Here, that is.

Fizz You said I had a heart attack. You said——

Peter You did. It's just... You're—in a coma.

Fizz How disagreeable.

Peter It isn't your time. You should recover.

The Lights fade

Fizz Recover?

Peter You are supposed to live to be a hundred-and-two.

Fizz No. I absolutely refuse. I'll be senile.

Peter Actually, you remain alert to the end.

Fizz I don't want to be a hundred-and-two.

Frank You don't want to lose twenty-four years though, do you?

Fizz The worst years. I think I could miss the worst years.

Peter There isn't much time.

Fizz You mean... I have to go back?

Peter It's very unusual... A decision must be made.

Fizz Who makes this decision?

Peter You. But time is running out.

Fizz What do I have to do?

Peter Nothing. Just make a decision. Stay, or—go.

Fizz If I stay, what happens next?

Peter You arrive in the garden, ring the bell, and I collect you. It's very straightforward.

Fizz What do people usually do? Under these circumstances.

Peter It isn't usual. People either pass over, or they don't. I don't want to rush you, but...

Fizz (*slowly*) Let me get this right. I have a choice?

Peter You have a choice. To help you make the choice... We showed you a little of the past.

Frank Me, or...

Peter Precisely.

Fizz You mean... I go back alone?

Peter Frank is supposed to be here. You aren't.

Frank It's Hollywood all over again.

Fizz I don't... I don't think.

Frank I'm sorry, my darling, I shouldn't have said that.

Peter The decision is yours alone. You can go back... Or you can stay, but you must hurry. Time is running out.

The stage darkens. We now hear only voices. The bench is struck during the Black-out

Frank (*desperately*) Just a minute. There's something I must say! Fizz... I never stopped loving you.

Fizz I know that. What idiots we were.

Frank Till we meet again, my darling.

Fizz Wait! Please, I don't want to leave him.

Peter Are you sure? You only have one chance.

Frank It's what you always craved, Fizz. Fame, publicity. You'll make all the newspapers. Think of the coverage! You'll be on all the chat shows!

Fizz I don't want to leave him.

Peter If you're sure.

Fizz I am sure. I want to be with Frank. I don't want to go without Frank.

The Lights come up, with a sunshine effect. Bird-song is heard

Frank and Fizz are alone on stage. He stands by the table at which she sits

Frank Is that a bell?

Fizz What?

Frank There. On the table. Is it a bell?

Fizz (*puzzled*) Yes. How odd. I didn't notice it before.

Frank Don't be dramatic. It hasn't just appeared like a genie from a bottle. It was there earlier. I noticed it. Ring it.

Fizz (*scared*) Shall I?

Frank Well, what else is it for? (*Lightly*) If an angel with large wings and a halo comes in, we're in dead trouble.

Fizz Or a harp.

Frank If anyone comes in with a harp, you're the only one in trouble. That affair with the music man was supposed to be long over.

Fizz You're such a fool. I am an old lady! How many times do

I have to remind you? I haven't had an affair for... Oh, it must
be ten years.

Frank (*affronted*) Ten years! Good God! I thought it was twenty-
five at least. It's obscene, a woman of your age.

Fizz (*ringing the bell*) Shut up.

Black-out. A chorus of bird-song

CURTAIN

FURNITURE AND PROPERTY LIST

On stage: Table. *On it:* Teapot and teacups, bell
                Chair
                Bench

Off stage: Script (**Man**)
                Phone (**Man**)

Personal: **Girl:** telegram

LIGHTING PLOT

Property fittings required: nil
Exterior. The same setting throughout

To open: Overall daylight

Cue 1	**Fizz**: "Shut up." *Change lighting*	(Page 6)
Cue 2	**Frank**: "Service is dashed slow here." *Change lighting*	(Page 8)
Cue 3	**Frank** rings the bell loudly *Change lighting*	(Page 14)
Cue 4	**Peter**: "You should recover." *Fade lights*	(Page 18)
Cue 5	**Peter**: "Time is running out." *Fade to black-out*	(Page 19)
Cue 6	**Fizz**: "I don't want to go without Frank." *Bring up sunshine effect*	(Page 20)
Cue 7	**Fizz**: "Shut up." *Black-out*	(Page 21)

EFFECTS PLOT

Cue 1   As the Curtain rises   (Page 1)
Bird-song

Cue 2   **Fizz**: "It can't have been here long."   (Page 1)
Lark sings

Cue 3   **Frank**: "…a few days' peace and quiet?"   (Page 2)
Lark sings

Cue 4   **Frank**: "We're at…"   (Page 5)
More bird-song

Cue 5   **Fizz**: "Shut up."   (Page 6)
Chorus of bird-song

Cue 6   **Girl**: "So sure of himself!"   (Page 7)
Jolly brass band music; fade when ready

Cue 7   The Lights come up   (Page 20)
Bird-song

Cue 8   Black-out   (Page 21)
Chorus of bird-song